TRAINING MANUAL ON PEOPLE'S BIODIVERSITY REGISTER

By the same author

—Community Participation and Sustainable Forest Development : Global Perspective

—Ecotourism and Livelihoods: Capacity Building for Local Authorities

—Public People Private Partnership for Sustainable Forest Development

—प्रशिक्षण मार्गदर्शिका—ग्रामीण सामुदायिक जैवविविधता पंजी—जल जंगल जमीन बही

About the Author

A.K. Bhattacharya is an Indian Forest Service Officer of 1983 batch from Madhya Pradesh cadre. He is presently an Associate Professor and Conservator of Forests in Indian Institute of Forest Management, Bhopal, an autonomous organisation under the Ministry of Environment and Forests, Government of India.

Dr. Bhattacharya is Post Doctoral in Environmental Sciences and has contributed a large number of articles in national and international journals on a range of topics related to forestry and environment. He has also to his credit a book on *Kandhar Plane Hijack,* based on his own experience as a hostage.

His main contributions to the field of eco-tourism include organising capacity building workshops and training courses for the local authorities of the various concerned departments, communities and NGOs, extending professional support to the State Government for promotion of eco-tourism, supervising research works on eco-tourism related topics, and preparing Eco-tourism Management Plans for few protected areas.

TRAINING MANUAL
ON
PEOPLE'S BIODIVERSITY REGISTER

"Jal Jangal Jamin Register"

Bio-Diversity Conservation and Livelihood
Security through People's Participation

A.K. Bhattacharya, *IFS*

Conservator of Forests

CONCEPT PUBLISHING COMPANY, NEW DELHI-110059

Cataloging in Publication Data—DK
Courtesy: D.K. Agencies (P) Ltd. <docinfo@dkagencies.com>

Bhattacharya, A. K.

Training manual on people's biodiversity register : "Jal jangal jamin register" : bio-diversity conservation and livelihood security through people's participation / A.K. Bhattacharya.

p. cm.

Includes bibliographical references (p.)

ISBN 8180692434

1. Biological diversity conservation—India—Citizen participation—Handbooks, manuals, etc. I. Title.

DDC 333.951 609 54 21

ISBN 81-8069-243-4

First Published 2005

Published and Printed by
Ashok Kumar Mittal
Concept Publishing Company
A/15-16, Commercial Block, Mohan Garden
New Delhi (INDIA)

Phones : 25351460, 25351794
Fax : 091-11-25357103
Email : publishing@conceptpub.com

Foreword

"Conservation of the bio-diversity is essential for the sustainable development". This fact has been established and accepted through different deliberations at the national and international fora including UN Conference on Human Environment in Stockholm (1972), Rio Summit (1992), Convention on Bio-diversity, National policy on Bio-diversity (1999) and the MP Bio-diversity Strategy and Action Plan (2002). It is now well understood that bio-diversity is a part of our daily lives and constitutes resources upon which families, communities, nations and future generations depend, and thus bio-diversity is fundamental to the fulfilment of human needs.

People's involvement in the conservation of the bio-diversity has been globally accepted, mainly because the communities are the closest to the bio-diversity and their livelihood is directly linked with the bio-resources. At the same time, their rich knowledge of the bio-diversity will be very helpful in better management of the natural resources. The community-based management of the bio-resources has now become the central focus of the National and the State policies. Community participation can serve as an effective tool for the sustainable management of the bio-resources and community based bio-diversity conservation for livelihood security.

There is today an increasing recognition on many fronts of the need to involve people in planning, implementation and monitoring roles in the management of natural resources. It is manifest in the emphasis in the Convention on Biological

Diversity of respecting the conservation and sustainable use practices of local communities, and equitably sharing with them the benefits flowing from the use of their knowledge. In this endeavour of involving people in inventorying and monitoring of biodiversity and knowledge of its uses we can build upon a variety of experiences of forging an alliance between the scientific establishment, the government machinery and the knowledgeable people, or barefoot ecologists, in the field.

Village Level Community/People's Biodiversity Registers (PBRs) are documents of ongoing and traditional knowledge and practices of bio-resource use and conservation for its participatory planning and monitoring, especially in agricultural, forestry and fishery sectors to protect against its disuse (erosion) and misuse (bio-piracy). PBRs are documents of people's knowledge of biodiversity and their perceptions about conservation, including sustainable use. PBRs can also help in protecting Intellectual property rights of knowledge contributors as an evidence of prior art, as a basis for sharing with them resultant research and commercialisation benefits equitably.

Biodiversity register process basically tries to encourage local, eco-friendly practices by providing them social recognition, as a counter-balance to prevalent propaganda for the use of new seeds, drugs etc., which often destroy ecology and social equity. The registers may not be protected against misuse by keeping in local custody but can protect against disuse by publicising their claims. Willingly disclosed unique traditional knowledge/innovations of people, documented with their prior informed consent can be incorporated in the national innovations register for social recognition, token reward and value addition/commercialisation, besides exposure.

Trained villagers, often along with local school/college teachers-students and/or NGOs, at the level of villages compile the registers at the village/hamlet level. PBRs can further be synthesised at the level of *talukas*/blocks, districts, states and nation, as computerised databases, to provide the information to all, for monitoring and prospecting.

PBRs can be prepared and implemented with the Government support, under the Local Biodiversity Chronicles (LBCs) provision at the local Biodiversity Management Councils under the emerging the Indian Biological Diversity legislation. LBCs can help proposed local Biodiversity Funds to reward conserves of biodiversity, traditional heritage sites, promote micro-processing and marketing of ethnic produce as being eco-friendly etc.

The manual is an attempt to provide a broad framework for undertaking such a participatory effort at inventorying and monitoring of biodiversity, its management and knowledge of its uses. It visualizes the overall process as involving a series of twelve sequential activities. These activities have been discussed in some detail in different chapters of the manual. For each activity, the manual suggests inputs required to undertake that activity, the relevant tools and methodologies, how the outputs of that specific activity will relate to other activities and the nature of documentation of the outputs. The manual has been supplemented with explanations and figures to spell out the rationale and provide the scientific background for that activity. The manual also includes schedules and formats for collection of data and focus discussion. The manual will be a useful compendium for the practitioners in the field of community based biodiversity conservation.

Mohammad Hashim
Principal Chief
Conservator of Forests,
Madhya Pradesh

Preface

The training manual is an outcome of the research project on "Community based bio-resource conservation for the livelihood security". The manual has been developed for the capacity building of the local level knowledgeable persons, specially the youth. This has been designed mainly for two categories of target groups, first the trainers and the local authorities, and secondly the rural youth to help them to understand the process, the collection of the data on biodiversity, preparation of PBR and monitoring of the changes in the biodiversity.

The manual addresses the overall process and the series of activities involved, and suggests steps in some detail for inputs required to undertake these activities, the relevant tools and methodologies, how the outputs of that specific activity will relate to other activities and the nature of documentation of the outputs. The manual provides schedules and formats for collection of data and focus discussion. The manual visualizes the involvement of a wide range of agencies in the whole process of community based biodiversity conservation and attempts to address all of them: Science and technology institution, Educational institution, Government organization, Elected body, NGO, Community based organization, Individual technical expert, Local knowledgeable individual, Teacher, Student, Citizen. These agencies may be operating on a number of different spatial scales: Hamlet, Village, Panchayat, District, State, Country, or Global. The manual should serve as an effective field handbook and research tool for the practitioners and all the stakeholders in the field of community based biodiversity conservation.

Acknowledgements

The author appreciates the technical support of Ms. Mamuni, Researcher, for the development of the Manual and editorial support of Ms. Sarika, Researcher, for the preparation of manuscript.

Contents

Introduction

It has been very truly said that one must treat the resources of the earth not as an inheritance from our forefathers, but as if borrowed from our descendents. People would thus treat natural resources prudently only if they themselves feel a long term stake in the health and sustainability of the resource base.

People all-round the world depend on natural resources for their day-to-day life. For example, farmers build their huts from stones, mud and bamboo and thus they know proper management of the resources. Hence, they are practical ecologists, continually interacting with the natural world as they strive to make a living. Similarly, fisher folk, fishing India's streams and rivers know more than any other, including trained scientists of the ongoing changes in the water courses and their snail, crab, fish, fauna etc.

BOX-1

What is Biodiversity?

Biodiversity is a term used to define all the natural or artificial resources available to living and non-living organisms. It is a blanket term used for the natural biological wealth that under-guards human life and well-being. Thus biological diversity can be divided into three broad categories, namely, genetic, species, and ecosystems.

- *Genetic Diversity* : Genetic differences can be expressed through differences in body sizes, colours of roses, and the heat of different chili and peppers.
- *Species Diversity* : This means the variety of different species in a particular habitat area, such as the abundance of fish, coral, and other species around the Great Barrier Reef.
- *Ecosystem Diversity* : This means the variety of different habitat, like grassland, forest ecosystem etc. (Figure 1)

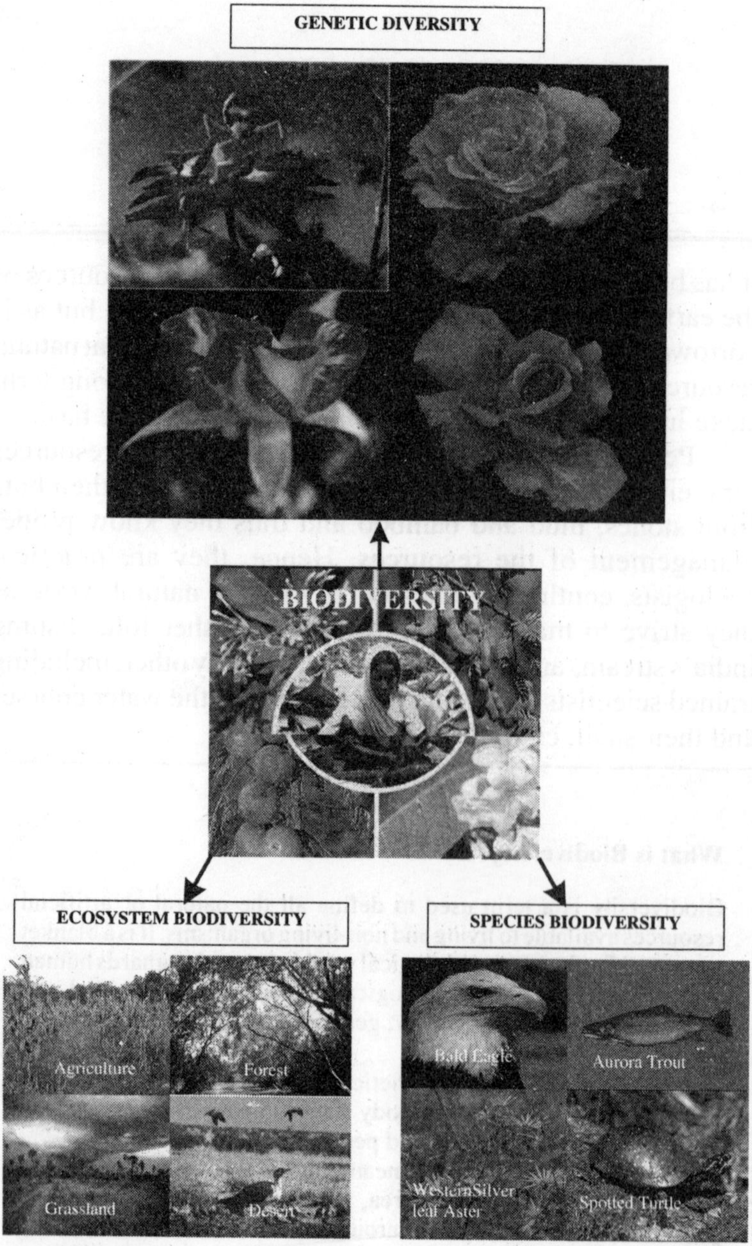
GENETIC DIVERSITY
BIODIVERSITY
ECOSYSTEM BIODIVERSITY
SPECIES BIODIVERSITY
Agriculture
Forest
Grassland
Desert
Bald Eagle
Aurora Trout
WesternSilver leaf Aster
Spotted Turtle

Figure 1

BOX 2

Why Biodiversity Conservation?

In recent years, loss of ecologically important species due to destructive human activities and their encroachment to natural habitats has been occurring at unprecedented rates. The extinction of each species brings the direct negative change in the environment, which shows direct effect on living beings. Hence to overcome this negative effect there is an urgent need to conserve the remaining biodiversity.

Biodiversity affords a "life support system". That means it provides direct benefits like food, fodder and clothes. Biodiversity is required for the recycling of essential elements, such as carbon, oxygen, and nitrogen. It is also responsible for mitigating pollution, protecting watersheds, and combating soil erosion. Since biodiversity acts as a buffer against excessive variations in weather and climate, therefore, it protects us from unfavourable events beyond human control. Biodiversity plays many more roles which affects positively both living and non-living beings.

The motivation and this knowledge are today ignored, slighted, and in consequence fast disappearing. Hence there is an urgent need to create institutions and mechanisms for actively involving local communities in affective management of Natural Resources, encouraging their traditions of conservation of biological diversity and recording and putting to good use their practical ecological knowledge. The initiative of the People's Biodiversity Register (PBR) is an attempt in this direction.

OBJECTIVES OF THE MANUAL

Think globally and act locally. This principle has been found to be the most effective undercurrent for the sustainable management of the local natural resources. It is considered that sustainable management of the bio-diversity can be effective only through indigenous knowledge, indigenous resources and indigenous technology. Based on the recommendations of the Convention on the National Policy and Macro-level Action strategy on Bio-diversity was formulated in 1999 by the Government of India, Ministry of Forest and Environment, New Delhi, and Madhya Pradesh Bio-diversity Strategy and Action Plan (2002) has been formulated by Government of MP, Ministry of Bio-diversity and Bio-technology, Bhopal. The main objectives are to:

— ensure conservation and sustainable use of biological resources.
— secure participation of State Government, communities, people, NGOs etc. in above activities.

BOX 3

People's Biodiversity Register

This programme had its origin in the Medicinal Plants Conservation Projects of Foundation for Revitalization of Local Health Traditions (FRLHT) and Western Ghats Biodiversity Network coordinated through Centre for Ecological Sciences, Indian Institute of Science, Bangalore.
The People's Biodiversity Register is expected to serve as a tool to—

(a) document, monitor and provide information for sustainable management of local biodiversity resources.
(b) promote biodiversity-friendly development in the emerging process of decentralized management of natural resources.
(c) establish claims of individuals and local communities over knowledge and such resources.
(d) perpetuate and promote the development of practical ecological knowledge of local communities and of traditional sciences such as Ayurveda and Unani medicines.
(e) teach environment and biology.

— help realize the consumptive and non-consumptive value of bio-diversity.
— ensure flow of benefits to the State as well the local communities.

The overall aim of the training manual is—

> "Conservation of the bio-diversity of the area and use them for the livelihood security and sustainable development of the area utilizing the human, social, physical and ecological assets."

The specific objectives are as follows—

- Documentation of the traditional knowledge of the bio-resources of the area including past history.
- Documentation of the existing bio-diversity, specially the endangered species through the local communities.
- Examination of the existing conservation practices and their effects.
- Identification of the strengths, weaknesses and negative factors for the bio-diversity conservation in the area.
- Analysis of potential of the livelihood through bio-resources.
- Analysis of potential for *in situ* and *ex situ* conservation
- Identification of training needs.
- Identification of management options.

EXPECTED OUTCOME

The training is expected to yield following outcome—

— Document on bio-diversity of the project area through CBR/PBR.
— Module for Community bio-diversity survey which can be replicated elsewhere.

— Awareness among people of project area about bio-diversity.
— Basis for developing livelihood option through the bio-diversity from this project area.
— Framework for bio-diversity audit.

HOW TO USE THIS MANUAL?

This illustrated manual provides a simple approach to understand the task given in the manual and how to fulfil those tasks. For fulfilling the task, steps have been given which will make the work easy. This enables the users to understand the meaning and essence of each task. The main objective of this booklet is to develop a clear understanding of biodiversity and how to approach for each and every task of its conservation.

Before following the steps illustrated in the following sections (1-12), at first go through the steps slowly to understand it properly and then discuss the steps. Afterwards apply it step by step as given under each chapter.

1

Identification of Target Species or Groups of Species

Method

Local knowledgeable individuals including local youth will be involved to identify and categorize the species according to their subsistence, commercial, nuisance and cultural importance.

Steps

1. Meeting the local people in Gram Sabha or conducting a separate meeting.

    (a) Gather the people of village or of the area, which has to be covered under PBR.
    (b) Or use Participatory Rural Appraisal (PRA)/Rapid Rural Appraisal (RRA) for developing a rapport with local people. (Refer boxes 4 and 5).

2. Explaining them the purpose of conducting meeting (Figure 2).
3. Analyzing the knowledge of people through different types of activities (refer box-6).
4. Selecting the knowledgeable individuals and some local youth that can be involved to identify and categorize the species.
5. Explaining them their work and then dividing them into groups.

Figure 2: Local People Conducting Meeting and Presence of a Urban People or Student Facilitating the Meeting

Figure 3: Participatory Planning for Biodiversity Utilization—Rapid Rural Appraisal

BOX 4

What is Participatory Rural Appraisal (PRA)/Rapid Rural Appraisal (RRA)? (Figure 3)

- *A typical PRA activity involves a team of people working for two to three weeks on workshop, discussions, analyses, and fieldwork.*
- *PRA techniques can be combined in a number of different ways, depending on the topics under investigation. Some general rules of thumb, however, are useful. Mapping and modelling are good techniques to start with, because they involve several people, stimulate much discussions and enthusiasm, provide the PRA team with an overview of the area, and deal with non-controversial information.*
- *RRA is more commonly described as a systematic but semi-structured activity out in the field by a multidisciplinary team and is designed to obtain new information and to formulate new hypotheses about rural life.*

BOX 5

Different tools of PRA/RRA

- *Transect walks and direct observations.* These are systematic walks with the villagers through the area of interest, observing, asking, listening, looking, and seeking problems and solutions. The findings can be mapped on a transect diagram. Most transect walks result in the outsiders discovering surprising local practices such as indigenous conservation practices, multiple uses of plants, and a great variety of crops.
- *Participatory mapping.* This involves constructing maps, on the ground or on paper, using materials such as sticks, stones, grasses, wood, tree leaves, coloured sands and soils, 'rangoli' powders, coloured chalk, pens, paper etc. As maps take shape, more people become involved, and so want to contribute and make sequential changes. There are many types of maps: resource maps of catchments, villages, forests, fields, farms, home gardens; social maps of residential areas of a village; impact monitoring maps, where villagers record or map pest incidence, input usage, weed distribution, soil quality, and so forth. Some of the most illuminating maps combine historical views with those of the present.
- *Time lines.* Historical analyses have been found to be a good icebreaker for field exercises and include detailed accounts of the past, of how things have changed, particularly focusing on relationships and trends. These include technology histories and review, crop histories and biographies, livestock breed histories, labour availability, trees and forest histories, education change, and population change.
- *Seasonal calendars.* Seasonal constraints and opportunities can be diagrammed month by month throughout the year. Ceremonies can be used as a crosscheck so that the names of months are validated and agreed upon. For this method people like pieces of stick, draw histograms in the dust or with chalk, or make piles of stones, seeds, or powders to represent relative quantities and patterns of rainfall, soil moisture, crops, labour, food consumption, illnesses, prices, animal fodder, fuel, migration, pests, income, expenditure, debt, children's games, and so on. Seasonal calendars can be drawn in linear fashion with twelve months to show a typical year or eighteen months to illustrate changes between years, or they can be drawn in a circle.

BOX 6

Appreciative enquiry—analysing strengths

Activity-1: Identifying Skill

Objective: To identify the more knowledgeable persons in the village.

Steps

1. Go around the area from where the data have to be collected.
2. Collect at least 10 different leaves, flowers or fruits.
3. Show these to the local people and ask them to recognize.
4. If anyone recognizes, then ask their different uses and its importance.
5. Collect those specimens only, which are known to you.

Activity-2: Discovery

Objective: To know about the strengths and weaknesses of the group of people or a person in the village. This activity generates new enthusiasm in the villagers.

Steps

1. In first round, tell a story of any person among yourself. In that story speak about his/her strengths, weaknesses and capabilities.
2. Then ask few questions from the people about their good experiences in the life.
3. Discuss about that person's good experience.
4. During discussion try to observe the capabilities of the local people.
5. Write down those strengths and capabilities and during data collection time make use of those capabilities.
6. Also, while during this work find out the capable persons who can help in recognizing the species and telling the local level importance of the species.

contd.

Box 6 (contd.)

Activity-3: Knowing the Resources

Objective: To know who is more knowledgeable about their surroundings.

Steps

1. Take the villagers to the nearabout areas and ask them to go and collect individually two to three materials which are lying on the ground.
2. For this at least 5 minutes should be given.
3. The collection site should be within a radius of 1 km, so that time is not wasted in wandering around. Specify the area for activity.
4. Such materials have to be collected which are lying down on the ground.
5. When everyone comes back with two materials each in their hand or whatever they collected, ask them to speak why they have collected that material and what is the importance of that material in their life. Or just ask them to tell general importance and significance.

6. Making use of their knowledge in identifying the species in field area.

2

Ascertaining Scientific Names of the Target Set of Species

Method

With the help of scientific and technical experts.

Steps

1. Species should be collected with the help of local people, and their herbarium should be made with the help of students involved in the team. (Refer Boxes 7 and 8).

BOX 7

How to prepare Herbarium?

(a) Herbarium is a collection of carefully dried plants. For making a herbarium of the collected plants, materials used/needed are—
   - A pile of old newspapers
   - At least four sheets of heavy cardboard, about 12×24 inches
   - Two or three old bricks or other heavy weights
   - 3×5-inch or 4×6-inch index cards and pencils
   - Scissors for cutting samples of leaves
   - Sheets of thin white cardboard (like shirt boards)
   - File folders
   - White school glue
   - A roll of wax paper

(b) When the plants or leaves are as big as they get at maturity, collect a sample. For leaves, including leaves from trees, cut or break a small group of leaves together. You can even collect small branches with flowers on them, too.

(c) For each sample, write down the date, the kind of plant, the location and collector's name on a 3×5 or 4×6 inches card and keep it with the sample (Figure 4).

BOX 8

How to preserve the specimen collected?

- For a sample collected, find a safe place on a shelf or bench to leave your sample for several days to dry. The area should have good air circulation to carry away moisture.
- Place two layers of heavy cardboard on the shelf or bench and then spread out some old newspapers on the cardboard. And put one sample between about a dozen layers of newspaper. Don't cover up each sample until you've included your 3×5 card with the leaves.
- Lay down another layer of about a dozen pieces of newspaper on top of each sample. Once you have all of your leaf samples stacked up, put another layer of newspapers on top, and then the other two sheets of heavy cardboard. Put the bricks or other weights on top of the cardboard.
- Leave the stack along for at least a week. After a week, take the top of the stack apart and look at the first layer of leaves. After they became very dry then you're ready to mount the leaves on the white cardboard. If your leaves aren't dry yet, then take apart the whole stack and put it back together again with new dry newspapers. Be sure to handle your leaves carefully, and keep your index cards with the right sample. Leave the stack again for some day, and then take a look again. Once again, if the samples are dry, remove from the newspaper carefully. And if sample are not dried then again keep it for drying.
- Spread a sheet of newspaper on top of a flat surface like a table, and then place a sheet of wax paper on top of the newspaper. Spread a few drops of white glue onto the wax paper, and spread it around until it's a thin, even layer a little bigger than your leaf sample. Decide which side of your leaf sample you'd like to have facing up, and then turn it so that the final "up" side is actually facing up.
- Gently set the leaf sample on top of your layer of white glue and let it set there for a few moments. Then gently lift it off again and lay it down, with the glue facing down, on your white cardboard. Place a little white glue in one corner of your white cardboard sheet, and glue down your index card, too, so that your leaf specimen will always have its original information with it.
- Once the glue is dry, your plant will last for years and years on its cardboard sheet.
- Keep each species, or kind, of plant in its own file folder, and store in a place where they will stay cool, dry and flat. Remember that they are still plants, and so if they get moist they can rot, or if they are found by insects or mice they will be got eatten.

2. Herbarium should be preserved carefully and then with the help of scientific and technical experts, the scientific names of species should be ascertained.
3. Then a list should be made which should have both the local and the scientific names.
4. In the list, species should be divided according to their subsistence, commercial, nuisance and cultural importance.

List of Target Species Collected

Name of target species collected				Importance of Target Species			
S. No.	Local Name of species (as used by local people)	Common Name (As used in general)	Scientific Name of Species (as given by experts)	Subsistence	Commercial	Nuisance	Cultural
1							
2							
3							
4							

Figure 4: Herbarium Sheet labelling

Genus Species Epithet	:	Clerodendron siphonanthus
Authority		Brandis Gamble Man
Vernacular name	:	Chingari
Location	:	Bagoha village location; Comptt No. RF412, Bagoha Beat, Kheri Range
Collector	:	Garib Das
Collection#	:	S512
Habitat	:	Grasslands; Clayey soil, dry
Habit	:	Shrub
Height	:	4-8 feet
Flower/Fruit colour	:	White/Dark blue
Date Collected	:	6 March 2005

3

Develop Resource Material and Build Human Capacity for Proper Identification of Target Set of Species

Method

The main emphasis of the training will stress on providing knowledge to the local educated youth for the documentation work. For this purpose, a format for documentation has been prepared. This will be filled by them with help of the identified knowledgeable people. It has been observed in the preliminary research that the local resource persons are well equipped with knowledge of the target species and the landscape. Therefore, no formal training is required for them.

Steps

1. To achieve target of chapter 3, training of students and forest staff is necessary.
2. No training is required for local knowledgeable people including women since they are well equipped with knowledge of the target species and the landscape as the local people deal with those natural resources in day-to-day life.
3. For Students and Forest Staff only a short duration training is required for certain purpose which are as follows—

(a) How to make herbarium?
(b) Which all activities should be taken?
(c) How to motivate local people for their involvement in work?
(d) How to provide knowledge to the students and forest staff for the documentation of biodiversity found in the field area?

4

Decide the Boundaries of the Study Locality

Method

Every village has its own *Gram Vikas Pustika* (Village Development Booklet), which includes all the required information of the village including its boundary.

Steps

1. To decide the boundaries of the study locality local people should be concerned.
2. Area demarcation can be based on administrative considerations and coincide with Panchayat boundaries.
3. For demarcation of boundaries in case of tribal hamlets within forest, Forest Range boundaries can be considered.
4. As the PBR is concerned with the local people and their relation with natural resources, hence boundary demarcation should preferably be based on the resource catchments of human communities.

5

Ascertain Geographical Coordinates, Collect Maps, and Satellite Imagery for the Study Locality

Method

Information/documents to be obtained from the Park/Forest officials and the Collector Office.

Steps

1. For deciding the boundaries of the field area, map of village or that particular area which has to be included in PBR, the relevant maps will be collected from Zila Parishad of the District, and/or Forest offices.
2. For ascertaining geographical coordinates, Global Positioning System (GPS) is needed and the students require a small training, to know how to operate this instrument.
3. GIS and Remote Sensing data of the respective area can be collected from NRSA, Hyderabad, or forest offices, if available.

6

Field Studies of the Occurrence and Appropriate Abundance of the Target Set of Species

Method

Quadrate method will be used for sampling of the field area.

Steps

1. To achieve this task students will be involved. And to know the abundance of the species Quadrate/line transect method will be adopted.
2. Quadrate/line transect method should be known by the students; hence the training will be imparted in this regard. (refer boxes 9 and 10)
3. Local individuals along with women should be involved in order to identify the species and their importance.

BOX 9

Line Transect Method (Figure 5)

A transect line can be made using a rope marked and numbered at 0.5m or 1m intervals.

The rope is then laid across the area you wish to study. The position of transect line is very important and it depends on the direction one wants to study. It should be thought about carefully before it is placed. Otherwise one may end up without clear results because the line has been wrongly placed. Hence it is worthwhile thinking about it before starting.

(contd.)

Box 9 (contd.)

A line transect is carried out by unrolling the transect line along the path identified. The species touching the line may be recorded along the whole length of the line (continuous sampling). Alternatively, the presence or absence of species at each marked point is recorded (systematic sampling). If the slope along transect line is measured as well, the results can then be inserted onto this profile.

Line Transect

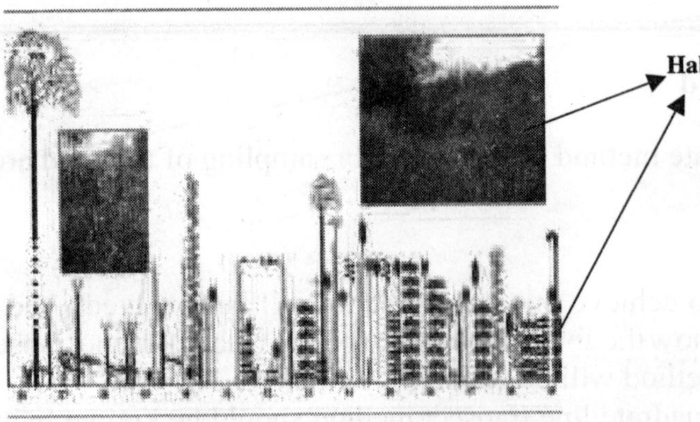

Figure 5

BOX 10

Quadrate Method (Figure 6)

Quadrates normally consist of a square frame, the most frequently used size being 1m^2 (see picture below). The purpose of using a quadrate is to enable comparable samples to be obtained from areas of consistent size and shape.

Choice of quadrate size depends to a large extent on the type of survey being conducted. For example, it would be difficult to gain any meaningful results using a 0.5m^2 quadrate in a study of a woodland canopy!

Small quadrates are much quicker to survey, but are likely to yield somewhat less reliable data than large ones. However, larger quadrates require more time and effort to examine properly. A balance is therefore necessary between what is ideal and what is practical.

As a general guideline, 0.5–1.0m^2 quadrates would be suggested for short grassland or dwarf heath, taller grasslands and shrubby habitats might require 2m quadrates, while quadrates of 20m^2 or larger would be needed for woodland habitats. At the other end of the scale, if you are sampling moss on a bank covered with a very diverse range of moss species, you might choose to use a 0.25m^2 quadrate.

To record percentage cover of species in a quadrate, look down on the quadrate from above and estimate the percentage cover occupied by each species. The estimation can be improved by dividing the quadrate into a grid of 100 squares each representing 1 per cent cover. This can either be done mentally by imagining 10 longitudinal and 10 horizontal lines of equal size superimposed on the quadrate, or physically by actually dividing the quadrate by means of string or wire attached to the frame at standard intervals. This is only practical if the vegetation in the area to be sampled is very short; otherwise the string/wire will hinder the lying down of the quadrate over the vegetation.

Quadrate Method

Quadrate

Figure 6

7

Validation of Information Collected in the Field on the Occurrence and Abundance of the Target Set of Species

Method

With the help of scientific and technical experts.

Steps

1. For the validation of the collected species, the expert should be taken into the field.
2. Or herbarium should be made of the collected target species and then those should be validated by the Scientific and technical experts.

8

Characterization of the Current Formal and Informal Management Regimes and Human Impacts on the Landscape/Waterscape and Target Set of Species

Method

Through discussion with the school teachers, *Gram Sabha* representatives, local *Panchayat* members and other leaders, government officials and scientific experts.

Steps

1. After validation of the data collected, the team member will try to characterize the management regimes and their impacts on the landscape/waterscape.
2. For characterization of the management regime and the impact of human on landscape/waterscape group discussion will be held.
3. Group Discussion with School teachers, local leaders, *Gram Sabha* members, Government officials, and scientific experts should be done separately (refer box-11).
4. Each and every point during the discussion should be noted, and then depending on the discussion, characterization of the management regimes and impact on landscape/waterscape should be done.

BOX 11

What is a group discussion? (Figure 7)

Group discussion is the way of bringing up the issue and then finding out the solution through the stakeholders.

A group discussion brings people together who share a common interest, goal, problem, or concern. The purpose is to discuss their feelings, observations, successes and failures around dealing with the specific topic. This discussion provides an opportunity to open their feelings in a healthy way and support others and themselves as each person is encouraged to share and openly express their honesty and truth around the topic.

How to conduct a Group Discussion?

The facilitator (means who conducts the discussion) sets the guidelines and makes sure that the group members understand them. The facilitator may decide on the topic to be discussed, however, a facilitator's main objective is to promote discussion and personal sharing by all group members.

Once the topic is stated or suggested by a group member, begin discussion by asking if anyone else has had a similar experience that they would like to share about. Don't answer questions brought up by the person sharing, even if you believe you have an answer, you can always take someone aside after group if you believe you have some information that would be helpful. Instead promote feedback from other members of the group (e.g. "What do you think?" or "Has this happened to anyone else?").

Always promote the group, the purpose is to share personal experiences only, identify when people are not sharing their personal experiences, encourage them to share their experiences. Identify speakers by asking if they have a personal experience they would like to add, or would they like to share, or comment on the topic.

In thenatural ambience (Forests)

In the technical atmosphere (Auditorium)

Figure 7: Group Discussion

9

Characterization of the Patterns of Ongoing Changes and Forces Driving Changes in Landscape/Waterscape, as well as Target Set of Species

Method

Through discussion with the school teachers, *Gram Sabha* representatives, local *Panchayat* members and other leaders, knowledgeable people, Government officials and scientific experts.

Steps

1. During discussion following points will be concentrated:

   (a) What are the ongoing changes taking places?
   (b) What are the driving forces which are causing such types of changes?

2. Changes can be positive or negative, for both the changes reasons will be examined. And for negative changes certain recommendations should be given and it should be tried to implement the recommendations.

3. In discussion school teachers, local leaders, *Gram Sabha* members, government officials, and scientific experts will be involved.

10

Designing a System for Managing All the Locally Collected Information as a Part for the Global Database

Method

With the help of scientific and technical experts.

Steps

1. All the primary and secondary data collected should be maintained properly in some register, so that if needed in future it can be utilized properly.

2. This database system can be maintained with the help of Scientific and Technical experts.

3. This database system should act as an ideal database for collecting the data in near future.

11

Reaching a Consensus on the Desired Patterns of Management of Landscape as well as Target Set of Species

Method

Discussions with the school teachers, *Gram Sabha* members, local *Panchayat* members and other leaders, knowledgeable people, Government officials and scientific experts.

Steps

1. After discussion with target groups separately, as mentioned in Chapters 8 and 9, particular type of management strategy should be developed to overcome the present management strategy for landscape/ waterscape.

2. This will be done in consultation with local knowledgeable people, scientific and technical experts.

12

Working Out a Plan of Management as well as Target Set of Species

Method

This has to be decided by the local people and the concerned government officials.

Steps

Both the steps mentioned in Chapter 11 will also be followed for fulfilling the Chapter 12.

Questionnaire

House-hold Information

1. Personal Information
   a. Name
   b. Age
   c. Caste
   d. Educational Qualification
   e. Occupation
   f. Number of Family members
      Men——
      Women——
      Children——
2. Comes under the user group of
   a. Farmer
   b. NTFP collector
      - Medicinal herb collector
      - Honey/bee collector
      - Other
   c. Fisherman
   d. Fuelwood collector
   e. Labours
   f. Businessmen
   g. Animal Husbandry
   h. Forest labour
   i. Others

3. User group data sheet

User Group	Activities	LSE Type	Species involved	Male/Female/ Children

4. List of the species used by user groups

Food	Fodder	Fuelwood	Medicinal Use	Cultural Use	Artisanal Use	Timber

5. Multiple use species

Species	Value of species/ why used	LSE	User group

6. Nuisance species

Species	Affected LSE and GES	Season of impact	Affected user group	Extent of Damage

LSE— Land Scape Element
GSE—Geographical Scape Element (group of two to three LSE will form one GSE)

7. Commercial Species

Species	Part sold	Price received (per kg)	Season	LSEs

8. Ownership, Usage and Access

LSEs	Ownership (State/Community/ Individual)	Usage (Fishing/Grazing/ Farming/Others)	Access (Open/Regulated Closed/ Unauthorized)

9. Species of the landscape element

(a) Type of Landscape Element = ________________

	Rare/abundant/ Common	Last when seen	What is the reason of extinction
Plants			
Tree			
Bushes			
Shrubs			
Herbs			
Grasses			
Parasites			
Epiphytes			
Climbers			
Birds			
Arboreal birds			
Cursorial birds			

	Rare/abundant/ Common	Last when seen	What is the reason of extinction
Animals			
Wild animals			
Domesticated			

10. Name of Species extinct

Species (Extinct)	How many years before they existed	Reason of their extinction

11. Name of Species Reduced or on the verge of extinction

Species (Reduced)	Reduction rate (More than 50% or less)	How many years ago they were abundant	Reason of their reduction	Present Management Activity done by user groups to stop the reduction	
				In situ	*Ex situ*

Focus Group Discussion Format

1. Mapping

A sketch map of the village showing the relative position of houses of people pursuing different resource use strategies along with important landscape elements like—pond, road, forest, habitation etc. While mapping use the local name to denote the main resources.

Locality and access details

1	Name of hamlet/settlement/ward	
2	Census code number	
3	Name of the revenue village of which the hamlet/settlement/wards is a part	
4	Name of the block/*Panchayat*	
5	*Taluka*	
6	District	
7	State	
8	PIN Code	
9	Altitude	
10	Longitude	
11	Latitude	
12	Number of Households	
13	Population	
14	Agricultural land	
	(a) Dry land	
	(b) Wet land	
	(c) Garden land	
	(d) Other crop land	

15	Waste land	
16	Grassland/Pasture	
17	Sacred Grove	
18	Water bodies (streams)	
19	Roads	
20	Human habitation/Buildings	
21	Total forest area	
22	Total geographical area	

2. To know the knowledgeable Local Individual (with respect to biodiversity)

Sl. No	Name of knowledgeable Individual	Community	Occupation	Special Knowledge/ Skill

3. To find out the user groups within the village

Sl. No	User Groups*	Community	Population

* User Groups—Group of people who depends on different types of resources

4. Livelihood strategies of different resource user groups making up the community

Sl. No.	Major basis of liveli-hood	Supple-mentary activities	No. of families	Resource user groups	Living and earth resources significant to livelihood strategies	Type of landscape elements harbouring the signi-ficant living and earth resources	Range of distance over which living and earth resources are acquired

5. Status of biodiversity in the resource catchment

Sl. No.	Local name of land-scape element (LSE)	Approximate area	Ow-ner-ship	Predominant Landuse pattern	Resource user groups involved	Other uses of LSE	Involve-ment of user groups from other commu-nities	Tradi-tional conven-tions or legal rights in usage of LSE

6. Status of Earth Resources

Sl. No	Earth Resources	Current status	Significant changes noticed in status of earth resources and their uses
1	Soil colour and texture		
2	Soil depth		
3	Productivity of soil and problematic soil		
4	Status of surface water		
5	Status of ground water		
6	Status of other earth resources like—sand, granite, etc. which have commercial value		

7. Status of Wild Plants

Sl. No.	Local name of the resource	Scientific Name	Specifically used by any other resource user group	Accession number in the herbarium	Part used	Purpose	Local availability status (rare, frequent, abundant)	Changes in the availability in recent times

8. Cultivated Plants

Sl. No.	Local name of the resource	Scientific Name	Specifically used by any other resource user group	Corresponding accession number in the herbarium	Part used	Cropping pattern and crop calendar	Local availability status (rare, frequent, abundant)	Changes in the availability in recent times

9. Wild Terrestrial animals, birds and invertebrates

Sl. No.	Local name of the resource	Scientific Name	Specifically used by any other resource user group	Accession number in the herbarium	Part used	Purpose	Local availability status (rare, frequent, abundant)	Changes in the availability in recent times

10. Domesticated animals, bird etc.

Sl. No.	Local name of the resource	Scientific Name	Specifically used by any other resource user group	Accession number in the herbarium	Part used	Name of the race/ breed	Purpose	Local availability status (rare, frequent, abundant)	Changes in the availability in recent times

11. Fish and other aquatic resources

Sl. No.	Local name of the resource	Scintific Name	Specifically used by any other resource user group	Accession number in in the museum	Part used	Purpose	Local availability status (rare, frequent, abundant)	Changes in the availability in recent times

12. Identify a significant historical event dating back to 30-40 years, in terms of transition in resource use patterns like dam construction, charcoal contractors, release of forest grazing land for cultivation, declaration of sanctuary etc. Provide brief information relating to such an event. For best result use Time-line method of Participatory Rural Appraisal (PRA).
13. Problems perceived regarding Landscape Element:

    (a) In continuing existing/current usage.
    (b) Conservation/promotion of biodiversity in Landscape element.
    (c) Priority of various resource users groups in solving the problems of LSE.

Resource user groups	Problems perceived	Solution suggested	To be implemented by

Bibliography

Achar, K.P. (1999). Documentation of People's Knowledge and Perceptions about Biodiversity and Conservation through People's Biodiversity Register at Mala Village Panchayat, Karkala Taluk (Karnataka), Biodiversity Conservation Prioritisation Project, Karnataka.

Anonymous, (1996). *People's Biodiversity Register—Recording India's Wealth.* Amruth, Bangalore.

Anonymous, (1995). *Community Biodiversity Register.* Centre for Ecological Sciences, Bangalore.

Bhattacharya, A.K. (2003). *Training Manual for "Jal Jangal Jamin Register" for Panna PBR Project.* Indian Institute of Forest Management, Bhopal.

Bhattacharya, A.K. (2004). Biodiversity based livelihood security : PBR based Project Report developed through the villagers of Bagoha, Narhi and Harsa of Panna District, Madhya Pradesh. Department of Biotechnology and Biodiversity.

Chambers, R. (1992). *Rural appraisal: rapid, relaxed and participatory.* Institute of Development Studies.

District Biodiversity Board, (2002). *District Biodiversity Initiative, 2002* (Jilla Jaiva Vividha Patal, 2002), Seoni, Madhya Pradesh.

Downes, David R. (1998). *Community Registries of Biodiversity Related Knowledge,* by and Sarah A Laird, UNCTAD Bitrade Initiatives.

Elliot, Charles (1999). *Locating the Energy for Change: An Introduction to Appreciative Enquiry.* International Institute for Sustainable Development. Winnipeg.

FAO (1999). Food security and biological diversity—The role of biological diversity in feeding the world. FAO document.

FRLHT (2001). *People's ecological planning (PEP) network.* Foundation for Rehabilitation of Local Health Traditions, Bangalore.

Gadgil, M., Acharya, S., Barman, R., Bhattacharji, P., Botre, S., Chhatre, A., Gandhi, K., Ganguli, A., Ghate, U., Kar, D., Mishra, M., Panigrahi, R., Pramod P., Rao P.R.S., Shrivastava, D.S., Vardhan, M. (1998). *Conservation: Where are the people?* The Hindu Survey of the Environment: 107-137.

Ghate, Utkarsh (1999). Access and Benefit Sharing (ABS) initiatives for Indian Biodiversity, *FRLHT,* Bangalore.

Ghate, Utkarsh (2000). Simple Village BIODIVERSITY REGISTER for sustainable use: Background, Methodology, Format and Follow Up. *FRLHT,* Bangalore.

Ghate, Utkarsh (2001). People's Biodiversity Register, *FRLHT,* Bangalore.

IIS (1999). *SRUSHTIGYAAN—A Methodology Manual for Documenting People's Priorities for Biodiversity and Conservation.* Centre for Ecological Sciences – Indian Institute of Science, Bangalore.

IIS (2000). *Participatory Local Level Assessment of Life Support System.* A Methodology Manual—Technical Report No.78. Centre for Ecological Sciences—Indian Institute of Sciences, Bangalore.

Lutz, Ernst and Julian Caldecott (Eds) (1998). Decentralisation and Biodiversity Conservation, World Bank.

Martin, G.J. (1995). *Ethnobotany: A method's manual.* Chapman and Hall, London.

Mukherjee, N. (1997). *Participatory Appraisal of Natural Resources.* Concept Publishing, New Delhi.

Ostrom, E. (1990). *Governing the commons: the evolution of institutions for collective action.* Cambridge University Press, New York.

Participatory Local Level Assessment of Life Support System. A Methodology Manual—Technical Report No.78. Centre for Ecological Sciences—Indian Institute of Sciences, Bangalore.

Posey, D. & Dutfield, G. (1996). *Beyond Intellectual Property: Towards Traditional Resource Rights for Indigenous Peoples and Local Communities.* IDRC (International Development Research Centre). Ottawa. pp. XV, 303.

Sahai, Suman (2000). *Indigenous knowledge confers rights on communities.* Asia-Pacific Regional Consultation on PGR.

Sarin, M. (1996). *Joint Forest Management: The Haryana experience.* Center for Environmental Education, Ahmedabad.

Singh, K. (1994). *Managing the common pool resources.* Oxford University Press, Delhi.

World Bank (2000). *Indigenous peoples, forests, and the World Bank: Policies and Practice.* World Bank Paper.

Relevant websites

http://www.howe.k12.ok.us/~jimaskew/botcolet.htm
http://www.offwell.free-online.co.uk/howto.htm
http://csdl.tamu.edu/FLORA/tfplab/labels.htm
http://www.fao.org/docrep/W3241E/w3241e09.htm#RRA definition
http://www.fao.org/docrep/W5830E/w5830e08.htm#participatory methods
http://www.livelihoods.org/post/Docs/biolive.pdf
http://www.offwell.free-online.co.uk/3howto.htm
http://www.rom.on.ca/ontario/risk.php?doc_type=listall &region=4

List of Resource Organisations/Persons

Prof. Madhav Gadgil
Centre for Ecological Sciences
Indian Institute of Science
Bangalore 560012, India
Telefax: +91-80-3601453
Email: <madhav@ces.iisc.ernet.in>
Website: http://ces.iisc.ernet.in/hpg/cesmg

Ms. Vidya Nayak
Nagarika Seva Trust,
P.O. Guruvayanakere,
Dakshina Kannada,
574 217, Karnataka, India
Telefax.: +91-08256-302019/ 302709
Email: <nstgkere@sancharnet.in>

Mr. P.V. Satheesh
Deccan Development Society (DDS),
H.No.1-11-242/1, Street No.5,
Flat No. 101, Kishan Residency,
Shyamlal Building Area,
Begumpet, Hyderabad - 500 016, India
Ph: +91-40- 7764577, 7764722/44
Email: <ddsppvr@hd2.dot.net.in>
Website: www.ddsindia.org

Ms. Vanaja Ramprasad
Green Foundation,
83 A, Srinatha Nilaya, 3rd Cross,
5th Main, BTM 2nd Stage,
Bangalore, 560 076.
Karnataka, India
Ph. 080- 678 45 09
Fax: 659 17 29
Email: <greenfound@tatanova.com>
Website: www.greenconserve.org

Mr. Ashish Kothari
Kalpavriksh,
Apt. 5 Shree Datta Krupa
908 Deccan Gymkhana,
Pune 411004, India
Tel/fax: 91-20-5654239
Email: ashish@nda.vsnl.net.in
Website: www.kalpavriksha.org

Dr. Suman Sahai
J - 235/A, Sainik Farms,
Khanpur, New Delhi,
110 062 India
Ph: +91-11-6517248/6856841
Fax: +91-11-6965961
Email: <genecamp@vsnl.com>
Website: www.genecampaign.org

Ms. Madhu Sarin
48, Sector 4, Chandigarh,
160001, India
Tel: +91-172-741429/740339/742417
Fax: +91-172-741135
Email: <msarin@satyam.net.in>

Mr. Raghunandan Velankar
Research & Action in Natural Wealth Administration,
(RANWA), C-26/1;
Ketan Heights, Kothrud,
Pune, 411038,
India.
Ph.: +91-20-5446518
Fax: 5424426.
Email: ranwa@pn3.vsnl.net.in;
Website: www.ranwa.org

Dr. B.M.S. Rathore, IFS,
Conservator of Forests & Member Secretary,
MP Biodiversity Board, 3rd floor,
Beej Bhawan, Jail Road,
Arera Hills, Bhopal
Tel: 09425174602 (m), 07552430226 (r),
07556334504 (o)
E-mail: bms_r@yahoo.com

Dr. Utkarsh Ghate, FRLHT,
50, MSH Layout, 2nd Stage, 3rd Main, Anand Nagar,
Bangalore, 560 024, India.
Ph.: 91-80-3336909/3434465
Fax: 3334167.
Email: <g.utkarsh@frlht-india.org>;
Website: http://www.frlht-india.org

NOTES